W9-CFA-816

...ETH IN HIM SHOULD NOT PERISH,
WORLD, THAT HE GAVE HIS ONLY BE
...LD NOT PERISH, BUT HAVE EVERLAS
...HIS ONLY BEGOTTEN SON, THAT WI
...EVERLASTING LIFE. FOR GOD   SO L
THAT WHOSOEVER BELIEVETH IN H
GOD SO LOVED THE WORLD, THAT H
...VETH IN HIM SHOULD NOT PERISH,
WORLD, THAT HE GAVE HIS ONLY BE
...LD NOT PERISH, BUT HAVE EVERLAS
...HIS ONLY BEGOTTEN SON, THAT WI
...EVERLASTING LIFE. FOR GOD SO LO
THAT WHOSOEVER BELIEVETH IN H
GOD SO LOVED THE WORLD, THAT H
...VETH IN HIM SHOULD NOT PERISH,
...LD, THAT HE GAVE HIS ONLY BEGOTT
PERISH, BUT HAVE EVERLASTING LIFE
BEGOTTEN SON, THAT WHOSOEVER

TO

Shunta Grimsley

FROM

Macedonia youth Dept.

Dec. 2006

FOR GOD SO LOVED THE WORLD THAT HE GAVE
HIS ONLY BEGOTTEN SON, THAT WHOEVER BELIEVES IN HIM
SHOULD NOT PERISH BUT HAVE EVERLASTING LIFE.
—John 3:16 NKJV

©2006 Freeman-Smith, LLC.

All rights reserved. Except for brief quotations used in reviews, articles, or other media, no part of this book may be reproduced or transmitted in any form or by any means, electronic or mechanical, including photocopying, recording, or by information storage or retrieval system, without permission by the publisher.

Freeman-Smith, LLC.

Nashville, TN 37202

The quoted ideas expressed in this book (but not Scripture verses) are not, in all cases, exact quotations, as some have been edited for clarity and brevity. In all cases, the author has attempted to maintain the speaker's original intent. In some cases, quoted material for this book was obtained from secondary sources, primarily print media. While every effort was made to ensure the accuracy of these sources, the accuracy cannot be guaranteed. For additions, deletions, corrections, or clarifications in future editions of this text, please write Freeman-Smith, LLC.

Scripture quotations are taken from:

The Holy Bible, New King James Version (NKJV) Copyright © 1982 by Thomas Nelson, Inc. Used by permission.

The Holman Christian Standard Bible™ (Holman CSB) Copyright © 1999, 2000, 2001 by Holman Bible Publishers. Used by permission.

Front Cover Bible Verse John 3:16 Holman CSB.

Original Lettering ©2006 The AIM Group, Inc.

Cover Design by Kim Russell / Wahoo Designs

Page Layout by Bart Dawson

ISBN 1-58334-391-1

Printed in the United States of America

Jesus,

BLESSED BE
THE NAME

TABLE OF CONTENTS

EVETH IN HIM SHOULD NOT PERISH
WORLD, THAT HE GAVE HIS ONLY BE
ULD NOT PERISH, BUT HAVE EVERLA
E HIS ONLY BEGOTTEN SON, THAT W
E EVERLASTING LIFE. FOR GOD   SO L
, THAT WHOSOEVER BELIEVETH IN H
GOD SO LOVED THE WORLD, THAT I
EVETH IN HIM SHOULD NOT PERISH
WORLD, THAT HE GAVE HIS ONLY BE
ULD NOT PERISH, BUT HAVE EVERLAS
E HIS ONLY BEGOTTEN SON, THAT W
E EVERLASTING LIFE, FOR GOD SO LC
, THAT WHOSOEVER BELIEVETH IN H
GOD SO LOVED THE WORLD, THAT H
EVETH IN HIM SHOULD NOT PERISH
RLD, THAT HE GAVE HIS ONLY BEGOT
PERISH, BUT HAVE EVERLASTING LIF

BLESSED IS
HIS NAME

On the very first Christmas day, when God sent His Son to become the salvation of the world, He bestowed a gift that is beyond price and beyond human comprehension. The familiar words of John 3:16 remind us that our salvation is a blessing from God—offered freely as an outpouring of His infinite love.

All of us are imperfect, but when we welcome Christ into our hearts, we are saved by God's grace. This is the message and the meaning of Christmas.

As we prepare for the holiday season, we must remember that Christmas begins with Christ. And as we celebrate the birth of the Christ child, we should praise God for the gift of His Son—God's ultimate gift—Jesus, the salvation of the world.

Christmas is about a baby, born in a stable,
who changed the world forever.

John Maxwell

In every Christian, Christ lives again.
Every true believer is a return
to first-century Christianity.

Vance Havner

The most important part of Christmas
is the first six letters.

Anonymous

"And they shall call His name Immanuel,"
which is translated, "God with us."

Matthew 1:23 NKJV

Christmas means the beginning
of Christianity—
and a second chance
for the world.

—

Peter Marshall

If we could condense all the truths of Christmas
into only three words, these would be the words:
"God with us."

John MacArthur

The miracle of Christmas is not on 34th Street;
it's in Bethlehem.

Rick Warren

For unto us a Child is born, Unto us a Son is given;
And the government will be upon His shoulder.
And His name will be called Wonderful, Counselor,
Mighty God, Everlasting Father, Prince of Peace.

Isaiah 9:6 NKJV

Then let every heart keep Christmas within.
Christ's pity for sorrow,
Christ's hatred for sin,
Christ's care for the weakest,
Christ's courage for right,
Everywhere, everywhere,
Christmas tonight!

—

Phillips Brooks

On Christmas Day two thousand years ago, the birth of a tiny baby
in an obscure village in the Middle East was
God's supreme triumph of good over evil.

Charles Colson

Jesus: His name blossoms on the pages of history like
the flowers of a thousand springtimes in one bouquet.

R. G. Lee

Keep your face upturned to Christ as the flowers do
to the sun. Look, and your soul shall live and grow.

Hannah Whitall Smith

Jesus Christ is the same yesterday, today, and forever.
Hebrews 13:8 Holman CSB

A CHILD IS BORN

Two thousand years ago, in the tiny town of Bethlehem, God presented the world with an incalculable gift—that gift, of course, was the baby Jesus. During the Christmas season, we celebrate Christ's birth, His life, His sacrifice, and the victory that can be ours through Him.

Christ's message is a transforming message. May we carry that message to the world, not just on Christmas day, but on every day of the year. And may the Christmas spirit, which was born with a babe in Bethlehem, dwell forever in our hearts.

And it came to pass in those days that a decree went out from Caesar Augustus that all the world should be registered. This census first took place while Quirinius was governing Syria. So all went to be registered, everyone to his own city. Joseph also went up from Galilee, out of the city of Nazareth, into Judea, to the city of David, which is called Bethlehem, because he was of the house and lineage of David, to be registered with Mary, his betrothed wife, who was with child. So it was, that while they were there, the days were completed for her to be delivered. And she brought forth her firstborn Son, and wrapped Him in swaddling cloths, and laid Him in a manger, because there was no room for them in the inn. Now there were in the same country shepherds living out in the fields, keeping watch over their flock by night.

And behold, an angel of the Lord stood before them, and the glory of the Lord shone around them, and they were greatly afraid. Then the angel said to them, "Do not be afraid, for behold, I bring you good tidings of great joy which will be to all people. For there is born to you this day in the city of David a Savior, who is Christ the Lord. And this will be the sign to you: You will find a Babe wrapped in swaddling cloths, lying in a manger." And suddenly there was with the angel a multitude of the heavenly host praising God and saying: "Glory to God in the highest, And on earth peace, goodwill toward men!"

Luke 2:1-14 NKJV

The manger is a symbol of what can happen
when Jesus Christ resides inside us.
The ordinary suddenly becomes extraordinary.

Billy Hybels

The magic message of Christmas is that God gave us
so much more than we can possibly give back!

Norman Vincent Peale

For I am persuaded that neither death nor life,
nor angels nor rulers, nor things present, nor things to come,
nor powers, nor height, nor depth, nor any other created thing
will have the power to separate us from
the love of God that is in Christ Jesus our Lord!

Romans 8:38-39 Holman CSB

The birth of Jesus is the sunrise in the Bible.

—

Henry Van Dyke

Tell me the story of Jesus. Write on my heart
every word. Tell me the story most precious,
sweetest that ever was heard.

Fanny Crosby

Jesus Christ was born into this world, not from it.

Oswald Chambers

The whole meaning of Christmas can be
summed up in the miracle of Christ's birth.

Arthur Bryant

At the name of Jesus every knee should bow,
of those in heaven, and of those on earth, and of those under the earth,
and that every tongue should confess that
Jesus Christ is Lord, to the glory of God the Father.

Philippians 2:10-11 NKJV

The Son of God became man to enable men
to become sons of God.

C. S. Lewis

Just as Our Lord came into human history from outside,
so He must come into me from outside.
Have I allowed my personal human life to become
a "Bethlehem" for the Son of God?

Oswald Chambers

For God did not send His Son into the world that
He might judge the world, but that the world
might be saved through Him.

John 3:17 Holman CSB

Jesus Christ founded His Kingdom
on the weakest link of all: a Baby.

Oswald Chambers

The Son of God does not want to be seen and found
in heaven. Therefore he descended from heaven
to this earth and came to us in our flesh.

Martin Luther

The old message "For unto you is born this day in
the city of David a Savior which is Christ the Lord"
is still the heart of Christmas.

Peter Marshall

For the Son of Man has come to save the lost.
Matthew 18:11 Holman CSB

WORSHIPPING THE CHRIST CHILD

*N*othing should obscure the fact that Christmastime is the annual birthday celebration of the Christian faith. Christmas day is, above all else, a religious holiday—a time for Christians everywhere to rejoice, to pray, and to worship God.

The 25th day of December, like every other day of the year, provides countless opportunities to put God where He belongs: at the center of our lives. When we do so, we are blessed.

During this holiday season, it is proper that we keep our eyes, our voices, and our hearts lifted upward as we offer profound thanksgiving to God through our worship and our praise.

Worship is wonder, love, and praise.
Not only does it cause us to contemplate
and appreciate our holy God, but it gives us vitality,
vigor, and a desire to obey Him.

Franklin Graham

The time for universal praise is sure to come some day.
Let us begin to do our part now.

Hannah Whitall Smith

All the earth shall worship You And sing praises to You;
They shall sing praises to Your name.

Psalm 66:4 NKJV

What a paradox that a babe in a manger should be called mighty!
Yet even as a babe, Jesus Christ was
the center of power. His birth affected the heavens
and caused a dazzling star to appear.
Midnight became midday as the glory of the Lord appeared to men.

Warren Wiersbe

This is the secret to a lifestyle of worship—
doing everything as if you were doing it for Jesus.

Rick Warren

I rejoiced with those who said to me,
"Let us go to the house of the Lord."

Psalm 122:1 Holman CSB

The fact that we were created to enjoy God
and to worship him forever is etched upon our souls.

Jim Cymbala

Praise and thank God for who He is
and for what He has done for you.

Billy Graham

Praise Him! Praise Him! Tell of His excellent greatness.
Praise Him! Praise Him! Ever in joyful song!

Fanny Crosby

Praise the Lord! Oh, give thanks to the Lord, for He is good!
For His mercy endures forever.

Psalm 106:1 NKJV

There's no better time than Christmas to become
the kind of seeker the wise men embodied.
Wise people still seek Christ.

Rick Warren

Worship is a voluntary act of gratitude offered
by the saved to the Savior, by the healed to the Healer,
by the delivered to the Deliverer.

Max Lucado

Therefore, through Him let us continually offer up
to God a sacrifice of praise, that is,
the fruit of our lips that confess His name.

Hebrews 13:15 Holman CSB

It is impossible to worship God and remain unchanged.

—

Henry Blackaby

SHARING CHRIST'S GIFTS

The old familiar hymn begins, "What a friend we have in Jesus." No truer words were ever penned. Christ showed enduring love by willingly sacrificing His own life so that we might have eternal life. As believers, we are blessed beyond measure—and God calls upon us to share our blessings.

Christmas is the season for giving, but gift-giving need not be synonymous with commercialism. The holiday season is the perfect time to share spiritual gifts as well as material ones. Spiritual gifts, of course, should take priority, but we must also give freely of our possessions, especially to those in need.

The words of Jesus are unambiguous: "Freely you have received, freely give" (Matthew 10:8 NKJV). May this holiday season, and every one hereafter, be a time when we, as followers of Christ, show our love for Him through the generosity that we show to others.

To celebrate the heart of Christmas
is to forget ourselves in the service of others.

Henry C. Link

Let us remember that the Christmas heart
is a giving heart, a wide-open heart that thinks
of others first. The birth of the baby Jesus stands as
the most significant event in all history because it has meant
the pouring into a sick world of the healing
medicine of love which has transformed all manner
of hearts for almost two thousand years.

George Matthew Adams

*Whatever you did for one of the least
of these brothers of Mine, you did for Me.*

Matthew 25:40 Holman CSB

What can I give him poor as I am; if I were a shepherd,
I would give him a lamb. If I were a wise man,
I would do my part. But what can I give him?
I will give him my heart.

Christina Rossetti

*So let each one give as he purposes in his heart,
not grudgingly or of necessity;
for God loves a cheerful giver.*

2 Corinthians 9:7 NKJV

This is Christmas, the real meaning of it:
God loving, searching, giving Himself to us;
man needing, receiving, giving himself to God.
Redemption's glorious exchange of gifts, without which
we cannot live, without which we cannot give
to those we love anything of lasting value.
This is the meaning of Christmas,
the wonder and the glory of it.

Ruth Bell Graham

Every time we love, every time we give, it's Christmas.

Dale Evans

The righteous give and don't hold back.

Proverbs 21:26 Holman CSB

Christmas is based on
an exchange of gifts;
the gift of God to man, his Son;
and the gift of man to God,
when we first give
ourselves to God.

—

Vance Havner

Abundant living means abundant giving.

E. Stanley Jones

A happy spirit takes the grind out of giving.
The grease of gusto frees the gears of generosity.

Charles Swindoll

The measure of a life, after all,
is not its duration but its donation.

Corrie ten Boom

*And may the Lord make you increase
and abound in love to one another and to all.*

1 Thessalonians 3:12 NKJV

SONGS OF CELEBRATION AND PRAISE

As we grow older, many things about Christmas change. But some things remain the same, including the songs that we sing. When it comes to Yuletide fare, our musical tastes are slow to change. Thank goodness.

The songs of Christmas, especially our favorite hymns, rank among the most beloved compositions ever penned. On the pages that follow, we celebrate a few of the songs we sing at Christmastime: may these holiday classics remain unchanged forever.

THE FIRST NOEL

The first Noel the angel did say
Was to certain poor shepherds in fields as they lay;
In fields as they lay, keeping their sheep,
On a cold winter's night that was so deep.

They looked up and saw a star
Shining in the east beyond them far,
And to the earth it gave great light,
And so it continued both day and night.

And by the light of that same star
Three wise men came from country far;
To seek for a king was their intent,
And to follow the star wherever it went.

This star drew nigh to the northwest,
O'er Bethlehem it took its rest,
And there it did both stop and stay
Right over the place where Jesus lay.

Then entered in those wise men three
Full reverently upon their knee,
and offered there in his presence
Their gold, and myrrh, and frankincense.

Then let us all with one accord
Sing praises to our heavenly Lord;
That hath made heaven and earth of naught,
And with his blood mankind hath bought.

—*Traditional English Carol*

GOD REST YOU MERRY GENTLEMEN

God rest you merry, gentlemen, let nothing you dismay,
Remember Christ our Savior was born on Christmas Day,
To save us all from Satan's pow'r when we were gone astray;

O tidings of comfort and joy, comfort and joy,
O tidings of comfort and joy.

From God our heavenly Father, a blessed angel came.
And unto certain shepherds, brought tidings of the same;
How that in Bethlehem was born the Son of God by name;

O tidings of comfort and joy, comfort and joy,
O tidings of comfort and joy.

—*Traditional 17th Century English Carol*

AWAY IN A MANGER

Away in a manger, no crib for a bed,
The little Lord Jesus lay down his sweet head.
The stars in the sky looked down where he lay,
The little Lord Jesus, asleep on the hay.

The cattle are lowing, the baby awakes,
But little Lord Jesus, no crying he makes.
I love Thee, Lord Jesus! Look down from the sky,
And stay by my cradle till morning is nigh.

Be near me, Lord Jesus, I ask Thee to stay
Close by me forever, and love me, I pray.
Bless all the dear children in thy tender care,
And take us to heaven, to live with Thee there.

—Anonymous

JOY TO THE WORLD

*Joy to the world! the Lord is come: Let earth
receive her King; Let every heart prepare him room,
And heaven and nature sing. And heaven and nature sing.
And heaven, and heaven, and nature sing.*

*Joy to the world! the Saviour reigns: Let men
their songs employ; While fields and floods, rocks, hills,
and plains Repeat the sounding joy. Repeat the sounding joy. Repeat,
repeat the sounding joy.*

*He rules the world with truth and grace,
And makes the nations prove The glories of his righteousness,
And wonders of his love. And wonders of his love.
And wonders, wonders of his love.*

—Words by Isaac Watts (1674-1748)

SILENT NIGHT

Silent Night! Holy Night! All is calm, all is bright.
Round yon virgin mother and child!
Holy infant so tender and mild,
Sleep in heavenly peace, sleep in heavenly peace.

Silent Night! Holy Night! Shepherds quake at the sight!
Glories stream from heaven afar,
Heavenly hosts sing Alleluia!
Christ the Savior is born! Christ the Savior is born!

Silent Night! Holy Night! Son of God, love's pure light;
Radiant beams from Thy holy face,
with the dawn of redeeming grace,
Jesus Lord, at Thy birth, Jesus Lord, at Thy birth.

—*Father Joseph Mohr, 1818*

O LITTLE TOWN OF BETHLEHEM

O little town of Bethlehem, how still we see thee lie,
Above thy deep and dreamless sleep, the silent stars go by;
Yet in thy dark streets shineth the everlasting Light,
The hopes and fears of all the years are met in thee tonight.

For Christ is born of Mary, and gathered all above,
While mortals sleep, the angels keep their watch of wondering love.
O morning stars, together proclaim the holy birth!
And praises sing to God the King, and peace to men on earth.

How silently, how silently, the wondrous gift is giv'n!
So God imparts to human hearts the blessings of His heav'n.
No ear may hear His coming, but in this world of sin,
Where meek souls will receive Him still, the dear Christ enters in.

O holy Child of Bethlehem! Descend to us we pray;
Cast out our sin and enter in, Be born in us today.
We hear the Christmas angels the great glad tidings tell;
O come to us abide with us, our Lord Emmanuel!

—*Phillips Brooks, 1868*

HARK! THE HERALD ANGELS SING

Hark! the herald angels sing,
"Glory to the newborn King.
Peace on earth and mercy mild;
God and sinners reconciled."
Joyful all ye nations rise.
Join the triumph of the skies;
with angelic host proclaim,
"Christ is born in Bethlehem!"
Hark! The herald angels sing,
"Glory to the newborn King."

—Charles Wesley, 1739

CELEBRATING GOD'S PROMISES

The words of Matthew 4:4 remind us that, "Man shall not live by bread alone, but by every word that proceeds from the mouth of God" (NKJV). During the season when we celebrate the birth of God's Son, we should study the Bible and meditate upon its meaning for our lives. Otherwise, we deprive ourselves of a priceless gift from our Creator.

God has given us the Holy Bible for the purpose of knowing His promises, His power, His commandments, His wisdom, His love, and His Son. As we study God's teachings and apply them to our lives, we live by the Word that shall never pass away.

The most important thing about the Bible
is that it points us to the living Word of God,
which is Jesus Christ.

Billy Graham

How do you wait upon the Lord?
First you must learn to sit at His feet
and take time to listen to His words.

Kay Arthur

The Holy Scriptures are our letters from home.

St. Augustine

But the word of the Lord endures forever.
And this is the word that was preached as the gospel to you.
1 Peter 1:25 Holman CSB

Nobody ever outgrows Scripture;
the book widens and deepens with our years.

C. H. Spurgeon

The Gospel is not so much a demand as it is an offer,
an offer of new life to man by the grace of God.

E. Stanley Jones

The only way we can understand the Bible
is by personal contact with the Living Word.

Oswald Chambers

Your word is a lamp to my feet and a light to my path.

Psalm 119:105 NKJV

When the child of God looks into the Word of God,
he sees the Son of God. And, he is transformed by
the Spirit of God to share in the glory of God.

Warren Wiersbe

The vigor of our spiritual lives will be in exact
proportion to the place held by the Bible
in our lives and in our thoughts.

George Mueller

*But He answered, "It is written: Man must not live
on bread alone, but on every word that comes
from the mouth of God."*

Matthew 4:4 Holman CSB

A SEASON OF CELEBRATION

The Christmas season is a time for joy and celebration. In the hamlet of Bethlehem, God gave the world a priceless gift: the Christ child. We, as believers, can rejoice: God, through His Son, has offered spiritual abundance and salvation to the world.

During our earthly existence, of course, we will all have trials and troubles—but as believers we are secure. God has promised us peace, joy, and eternal life. So, as we join in the celebrations of this sacred holiday, let us rejoice in God's most glorious gift: a baby born in a manger—a baby who forever changed the world. And then, with hope in our hearts and praise on our lips, let the celebration begin!

Blessed is the season which engages
the whole world in a celebration of love.

Hamilton Wright Mabie

Where the soul is full of peace and joy,
outward surroundings and circumstances are
of comparatively little account.

Hannah Whitall Smiith

Rejoice always, pray without ceasing,
in everything give thanks;
for this is the will of God in Christ Jesus for you.

1 Thessalonians 5:16-18 NKJV

Rejoice, that the immortal God is born,
so that mortal man may live in eternity.

Jan Hus

Christ and joy go together.

E. Stanley Jones

Joyful, joyful, we adore thee, God of glory,
Lord of love. Hearts unfold like flowers before thee;
opening to the sun above.

Henry Van Dyke

*This is the day the LORD has made;
we will rejoice and be glad in it.*

Psalm 118:24 NKJV

Claim the joy that is yours. Pray.
And know that your joy is used by God to reach others.

Kay Arthur

When we bring sunshine into the lives of others,
we're warmed by it ourselves.
When we spill a little happiness, it splashes on us.

Barbara Johnson

Go tell it on the mountain,
over the hills and everywhere.
Go tell it on the mountain, that Jesus Christ is born!

Traditional American Spiritual

Rejoice in the Lord always. I will say it again: Rejoice!

Philippians 4:4 Holman CSB

A TIME FOR FAMILY AND FRIENDS

*C*hristmas is a season when families gather to share food, songs, and stories. Holiday celebrations bring us together, and our traditions remind us of our heritage.

Christmas is a time for going home. And even when we can't enjoy the physical presence of family and friends, we can still find a special place for them in our hearts.

This holiday season, like every other, should be a time of thanksgiving and fellowship. And, amid the holiday happenings, let us always remember the One who came to earth so that we might have abundance and salvation. Jesus said, "As the Father loved Me, I also have loved you; abide in My love" (John 15:9 NKJV). He first loved us; let us return His love by sharing it.

Christmas is a day of meaning and traditions,
a special day spent in the warm circle
of family and friends.

Margaret Thatcher

A Christmas family-party!
We know of nothing in nature more delightful!

Charles Dickens

The Golden Rule begins at home.

Marie T. Freeman

Beloved, if God so loved us,
we also ought to love one another.

1 John 4:11 NKJV

I hope you will find a few folks who walk with God
to also walk with you through the seasons of your life.

John Eldredge

Living life with a consistent spiritual walk
deeply influences those we love most.

Vonette Bright

Live in the present and make the most of
your opportunities to enjoy your family and friends.

Barbara Johnson

Above all, put on love—the perfect bond of unity.
Colossians 3:14 Holman CSB

And now abide faith, hope, love, these three;
but the greatest of these is love.

—

1 Corinthians 13:13 NKJV

CHRISTMAS MEMORIES

*C*hristmas is a time for memories: revisiting old ones and making new ones. If we're lucky and wise, we do them both.

No season carries with it as many reminiscences as the holiday season. As December 25th approaches, we are confronted with a double dose of memory-evoking events: the end of another year and the passing of another Christmas. No wonder we find ourselves reflecting on the past.

This year, as we celebrate this holiday season and give thanks for the ones that have gone before, let us thank God for all His blessings: past, present, and future. And let us keep our happy memories of Christmases past forever in our hearts.

Happy, happy Christmas, that can win us back
to the delusions of our childhood days, recall to
the old man the pleasures of his youth, and transport
the traveler back to his own fireside and quiet home!

Charles Dickens

Line by line, moment by moment, special times
are etched into our memories in the permanent ink
of everlasting love in our relationships.

Gloria Gaither

Search for the Lord and for His strength;
seek His face always.
Remember the wonderful works He has done.

Psalm 105:4-5 Holman CSB

Christmas is a good time to take stock of our blessings.

Pat Boone

We recall the special Christmases that
are like little landmarks in a life of a family.

Marjorie Holmes

As another Christmas passes, the memory of it stays
and hovers like the scent of cedar. And even if
it can't be Christmas all the year, memories remain.

Minnie Pearl

I give thanks to my God for every remembrance of you.
Philippians 1:3 Holman CSB

During the Christmas season,
I hope that your own times
of excitement and sharing
and fellowship will leave you
with a special gift—
memories that will last a lifetime.

—

James Dobson

THE GIFT OF CHRIST'S LOVE

*T*he inescapable promise of Christmas is this: Christ loves us. Even though we are imperfect, fallible human beings, and even though we have fallen far short of God's commandments, Christ's love is perfect and steadfast.

As we accept Christ's love and honor His commandments, our lives bear testimony to His power and to His grace. Christ's love changes everything; may we, as believers, allow it to change everything in us.

We tend to focus our attention at Christmas on
the infancy of Christ. The greater truth of the holiday
is His deity. More astonishing than a baby
in the manger is the truth that this promised baby
is the omnipotent Creator of the heavens and the earth!

John MacArthur

If you're a thinking Christian,
you will be a joyful Christian.

Marie T. Freeman

Jesus: the proof of God's love.

Philip Yancey

*Greater love has no one than this,
than to lay down one's life for his friends.*

John 15:13 NKJV

If you come to Christ, you will always have the option
of an ever-present friend. You don't have to dial
long-distance. He'll be with you every step of the way.

Bill Hybels

Amazing Grace! How sweet the sound that saved
a wretch like me! I once was lost but now am found;
was blind, but now I see.

John Newton

Who can separate us from the love of Christ?
Can affliction or anguish or persecution or famine
or nakedness or danger or sword? . . . No, in all these things
we are more than victorious through Him who loved us.

Romans 8:35, 37 Holman CSB

Love came down at Christmas,
Love all lovely, Love divine;
Love was born at Christmas;
star and angels gave the sign.

—

Christina Rossetti

I have come that they may have life,
and that they may have it more abundantly.

John 10:10 NKJV

I have come as a light into the world,
so that everyone who believes in Me
would not remain in darkness.

John 12:46 Holman CSB

I am the door.
If anyone enters by Me, he will be saved.

John 10:9 NKJV

And remember, I am with you always,
to the end of the age.

Matthew 28:20 Holman CSB

At the name of Jesus every knee should bow,
of those in heaven, and of those on earth,
and of those under the earth,
and that every tongue should confess
that Jesus Christ is Lord,
to the glory of God the Father.

—

Philippians 2:10-11 NKJV

HAVE EVERLASTING LIFE. FOR GOD
TEN SON, THAT WHOSOEVER BELIEV
G LIFE. FOR GOD SO LOVED THE WO
OEVER BELIEVETH IN HIM SHOULD N
O THE WORLD, THAT HE GAVE HIS O
HOULD NOT PERISH, BUT HAVE EVER
AVE HIS ONLY BEGOTTEN SON, THAT
T HAVE EVERLASTING LIFE. FOR GOD
TEN SON, THAT WHOSOEVER BELIEV
G LIFE. FOR GOD SO LOVED THE WO
OEVER BELIEVETH IN HIM SHOULD B
THE WORLD, THAT HE GAVE HIS ON
HOULD NOT PERISH, BUT HAVE EVER
AVE HIS ONLY BEGOTTEN SON, THAT
T HAVE EVERLASTING LIFE. FOR GOD
SON, THAT WHOSOEVER BELIEVETH
R GOD SO LOVED THE WORLD, THA
IEVETH IN HIM SHOULD NOT PERIS